NOT SO GREEN AS CABBAGE LOOKING

RECOVERING FROM A STROKE
WITH A LITTLE GALLOWS HUMOR ALONG THE WAY

SIMON BARTON

iUniverse books may be ordered through booksellers or by contacting:

iUniverse
1663 Liberty Drive
Bloomington, IN 47403
www.iuniverse.com
1-800-Authors (1-800-288-4677)

ISBN: 978-1-5320-5290-3 (sc)
      978-1-5320-5291-0 (e)

Library of Congress Control Number: 2018910959

Print information available on the last page.

iUniverse rev. date: 03/04/2019

CONTENTS

"To Sarah.. Those trousers look way better on you than they ever did on me!

Foreword by
Maura English Silverman, MS,CCC/SLP

Sometimes understanding your role in someone's journey is not immediately known. Initial impressions, being what they are, can suggest only pieces to the puzzle, rough outlines of shapes that will reveal themselves as you share stories, compare backgrounds and impressions of what this relationship might hold.

Understanding that in my role as a speech pathologist, specifically, and a rehabilitation enthusiast, generally, I will be introduced to individuals as they stand along a forced Likert scale, at a point frozen in time from the life changing event that forced the introduction. The individual, being weeks, months or years from a catastrophic course change in their life, will be seeking knowledge, opinions, even detailed directions from someone who should know, who must know, what lies ahead and what to do to get to their destination, their goal. A responsibility that none of the rehabilitation professionals that I know take lightly. Without the benefit of a crystal ball or a recovery GPS mode, we lean on clinical outcome research, data from collective studies, theories and predictive variables about motivation, ...oh, and a whole lot of clinical gut feelings.

And sometimes we are challenged, taken to task by those whose lives are directly impacted by our professions of hope; our help in developing "realistic" goals and the clinical coaching that may be interpreted as canned, cautious explanations.

Meet Simon Barton… From the moment I met this incredibly sweet and self-deprecating genius from across the pond, I knew that he was going to challenge, teach and inspire me, as much, if not more, than I would have the honor to provide. "When, exactly, will I get better?" or "With all of the strokes that occur, there must be an algorithm for figuring it out by now" …probably paraphrasing, but definitely hitting the tone, Simon was consistently frustrated by the answers, or lack thereof, from those he saw as possessing the rehabilitation journey atlas.

This book, a collection of stories that reveal the unearthing of awareness, gradual and often painful acceptance of the impact of an insult to the master computer (even one of a dynamically creative inventor and engineer), has been as much of a therapeutic modality for Simon as any trick/tool up the average rehab therapist's sleeve. It is, as I have often preached, the marriage of engagement, determination, hope and purpose that brings one to full life participation.

Simon has always been quick to compliment and highlight the efforts of his peers, clearly inspired by their perseverance and commitment to the journey. But, with humility and characteristic politeness, he will deflect the praise he so truly deserves. This cathartic creation, from title to final impressions has given Simon the opportunity to see what we see, to know what we have known all along. The answer to the question about how far one will go, lies solely in the mindset and mission of the individual himself. Congratulations, Simon, on a work that humorously follows the path that you paved on your own. As far as this foreword-author is concerned, it's been an immense pleasure to cheer you on.

Because it's for you, I must end with a joke, a "pun" as you might call it. Not just any pun; but one that is slightly irreverent and ultimately laced with abundant kindness...just like you!

Maura: "Hey, Simon...did you hear about the guy who lost his whole left side?"

Simon: "No, Maura (aka Maude), what happened?"

Maura: "He's all right now"

You are more than "alright", Simon...you are one of my heroes. Much love, Maura

Unlike most animals, God gave us humans only two legs so that we could better learn how to rise up after a fall.

Preface:

I have to be careful NOT to contradict myself with the following prologue, but in all honesty, I was encouraged to write this book by my Speech Pathologist and hero, Maura, She felt that the simple act of writing things down will help me take ownership of my particular recovery process.. and certainly, I can concur, the exercise has had a tremendous and positive effect on me - but as the potential of a real and tangible book was looming, I really wanted to tell a story that emphasizes our natural (human) ability to evolve and recover mostly through self-awareness and not just because we need an expert in the field to tell us how to do it.

As you will see, I certainly did not have any answers which resulted in me making many mistakes from which I could learn, I can also confirm that many of the answers I (eventually) worked out for myself had actually been suggested to me previously by one of those experts I just (nearly) denounced! Be assured, I have no intention of unduly taking credit for the progress I have made single-handedly, quite the contrary, I am only saying that, for me, it was not until I figured it out for myself that what all the experts were saying made sense did I truly own it and see significant improvements to the overall recovery process.

Prologue:

The following account does not offer the reader any new or novel insights concerning Stroke, it certainly provides no cures. For the Stroke Survivor, it gives little to no comfort or hope that all will be well soon, it is simply an honest and frank account of how somebody's whole life (mine) and the closest lives around them (family) WILL BE TURNED UPSIDE DOWN almost to the point of destruction and the enormity of the task(s) ahead to endure it. In my case, however, to the dismay of the medical professionals around me, I did retain an ability to see the funny side of things and through a little humor, some self-deprecation, and a huge amount of support, I have managed to live with the consequences of Stroke and how, ultimately, all will be well in the end.. At the time of commencing this book, it has been three and a half years since the stroke impacted me, and so I still regard myself very much as a "work in progress" and through better understanding and continued reinvention, *I will* see this thing through, as everyone does in the end.

The title, "Not So Green as Cabbage Looking!" has a triple meaning in this case – it is an expression from the North of England equivalent to, "I am not just a pretty face" or, "I didn't just fall out of the stupid tree" and so on. A little while ago, my wife, Sarah, instinctively used the phrase one time when we were trying to remember an actor's name from an old movie and when I remembered the individual, "ah", she (impulsively) responded, "You are not so green as cabbage, afterall!" Secondly, it also holds some additional relevance because when she got to the Emergency Room where I was first admitted she was cautioned to prepare herself – apparently, the stroke was quite "massive" and even if I were to survive the next hour or two she was given the impression that there was a small possibility I might not be "all there" when I came too, some kind of "vegetable", she feared. Thirdly and finally, Physical and Occupational Therapists encourage their stroke patients to use a mirror for visible feedback of movement to help stimulate and re-train the brain but for the longest time, however, I did not care for, let alone recognize the person looking back at me.

It has taken a long time for me to learn to take the view it is just another chapter in my life, certainly not a good one, but one of the many we face, as we progress. Heck, perhaps we should think ourselves lucky... Afterall, not everyone gets to live through this ordeal, however horrendous it may be, it gives us an opportunity to re-examine our life, our character and make adjustments (in my case) for the better. Further, we also do not have to feel guilty parking in the closest space to the store - so I ask you, who are we to complain!?

The Main Event:

Tuesday, May 21, 2013 should have been an average day in the office, but with my eldest son, Josh, getting married at the end of the month, there was still some landscaping to do in preparation for the barbecue/reception for 150+ guests, so I took the morning off. This was not helped by the fact that my small business was going through some major "growing pains". Indeed, we were on course for doubling our sales over 2012. We had a huge order book, everything looked rosy, except we did not have the cash to support that level of growth and clearly, I was under much more stress than I needed at that time.

Socially, I liked a drink and smoke (although not to excess) and I mistakenly thought myself a pretty fit bloke. I spent much of my free time in the garden on various outdoor projects; and I played reasonably competitive tennis every week. Sure, I could get a little breathless chasing down a ball, but heck, I was 52 years old, what do you expect my age? So I saw little reason to interrupt my busy week by attending the (recommended, over-50) Medical/Physical my GP, Dr. Chatterjee kept on nagging about. For a relatively petite lady, she scared the bejeebers out of me, but somehow I always found a way to perpetually postpone the thing (us Brits are notorious for delaying doctor's medical appointments and deferring the Dentist until we die or at the very least, until our teeth fall out). Of course, if I knew what I know now, I would have moved the appointment higher up my priority list back in the spring of 2013.

My first job when getting to the office later that afternoon was to respond to the Bank's Agent, who left me a voicemail the previous day in respect of my application to refinance my existing home mortgage.

I placed the call with the Representative, a lady named Debbie. "Okay Mr. Barton", she said, "I just need to go over a few details with you...", "No problem, ask away", I replied. I remember at one point during the conversation, I was struggling to provide the answer for the date of my birth, which at the time I put down to the common problem of mixing up the month and day - for Europeans (and the rest of the world), the day and month is reversed. (9th of March, 1974, is referred 9-3-74, vs. the American system, 3-9-74). Instinctively, I answered, "8-7-60" but quickly corrected myself. "Hold on! In your language that would be 7-8-60, or, to be exact and let me repeat.. I was born on 8th July, 1960, I mean.. err, July 8th, 1960", for some reason, I just could not seem to get the message across or pronounce the date properly and with the absence of Debbie's response, tried to say it again and again but it just did not sound right. With hindsight, I think I was simply "slurring" my words, (one of those tell-tale signs of stroke; although at that time, I certainly had no idea I was in serious trouble). As I struggled to get the words out, I remember a strong sensation of dizziness which resulted in me, literally, falling out of my chair.

Ed, my Sales Manager, was the first to find me, lying on the floor of my office and a 911 call was placed immediately. My daughter, Hannah, the company's Marketing Manager, sat with me until the first responders arrived about 15 minutes later.

Apparently, Hannah told me

3

later, I was unable to speak at all and that the whole left side of my face had completely "drooped". She said I kept pointing to my face and waving my finger around, like I was trying to tell her something. It was clear to her even before the Medics arrived, that I likely suffered a Stroke of some kind.

When the First Responders did collect me, they also confirmed their suspicions and I was immediately whisked away to Rex Hospital's Emergency Department.

Fortunately for me, Rex had recently introduced a special emergency response program for in-bound

REX HOSPITAL

NURSE EILEEN

Expert on Stroke
See Me Before You Croak

Stroke victims. As I was coming round to what seemed at first, to be a chaotic scene, Nurse Eileen M (Rex's Stroke Program Coordinator) along with Dr. Sean T immediately took charge and stamped their authority on the following proceedings. After getting the necessary permission from my wife, Sarah, who managed to rush to the hospital in record time, I was treated with TPA (Tissue Plasminogen Activator), sometimes called a "clot-buster" drug – it is designed to do just that (so long as it is administered within 3-4 hours of the Stroke). Dr. Susan Glenn was the Neurologist on call that day and having examined the various imagery (MRI's, Scans, etc.), thought it best I spend the next

day or two in the ICU, until things settled down a bit – My excessively swelling brain, being her primary concern, apparently.

I really do not remember anything much about my stay at Rex or even the level of concern my condition held. - I was comatose much of the time.

I do attribute the speed of the first responders and the immediate and professional attention I received at Rex's Emergency Department as the primary reason why I am still above ground. But in addition, I have to believe that simply, it was not my time. There was more I needed to do.

Allegedly, when Sarah was told that I had suffered a brain injury she apparently responded with one blunt word: "impossible!".. "..and why do you say that?" asked the Doctor, "because he DOESN'T HAVE A BRAIN!" she replied.

Rehab Hospital Care:

After 10 days, it was felt that I could leave Rex's ICU department and be transferred to the well-regarded rehab facility headed by Dr. Mike Harris at nearby HadyMed Hospital.

Victims of Stroke can suffer quite varying disabilities with different levels of severity depending on the specific location of the injury and the length of time the brain was starved of oxygen, in my case, the damage was limited to an area to the right side of my brain which meant a subsequent loss of control to my left side limbs and most negatively affected, my left hamstring and Tibialis leg muscles, triceps and biceps in my left arm. Any use of my left hand and fingers was highly limited and frankly, non-existent. Nothing – nada!

At HadyMed, I was labeled a "Fall Risk" which meant that under no circumstances would I be allowed to try and get out of bed - even with the aid of a Nurse. Accordingly, I spent much of the day in bed - the most uncomfortable and unpleasant beds I have ever had the misfortune to lie upon. It was made worse by the fact that it used advanced technology to keep me there… Any effort I made to "escape" was monitored (not that it stopped me from trying) - before my toe even touched the ground a horrendous screeching alarm would go off through the headboard speakers shortly followed by a perturbed voice.. "Mr. Barton! I do hope you are NOT trying to get out of bed!?!" The alarm remained on until an inconvenienced and indignant nurse came in to turn it off. "Will you never learn, Mr. Barton?" (Heck, I only wanted to go to the restroom having never mastered the dreaded Urinal!)

I did feel the rigid rules associated with being a "fall risk" were a little bit harsh; getting in and out of bed and into the wheelchair would be managed only by the use of a "Hoyer" (a small crane). It seemed a lot more trouble than it was worth

but I must acknowledge that the nursing staff were extremely patient, truly amazing, very cheerful, and without exception, extremely supportive and helpful. Special mention goes to Nurse Suzanne H who, for the most part, somehow managed to keep me on the "straight and narrow" and tolerated my many misgivings. Nurse Cassie W was one of the few that was strong enough to maneuver me on her own when it was necessary.

I remember when she helped me dress one time, she pulled my underwear up with such force I was "dangling" 2 feet in the air - and I am not a small guy! This was followed by her commenting.. "I guess I gave you a wedgie, huh?" Despite having resided in

North Carolina for over 25 years, I had never heard the term before. The episode really did bring tears to my eyes and not so much from the discomfort but more from the uncontrollable giggling I couldn't keep back.

As luck would have it, the wife of my Manufacturing Manager, Debbie O, RN, happened to work at Hady-Med as a "Wound Care Specialist". And Debbie would kindly sit with me and bring me a cup of tea each morning, which for a Brit, is a great way to start the day! Tea makes you pee and of course, under normal circumstances I would have easy access to the loo but in my current condition, that meant more

practice and subsequent failure and embarrassment with the dreaded plastic urinal a little later on.

The Wedding:

It was fast approaching my son's wedding day. Family from the UK had arrived, and rather than taking the opportunity to catch up with each other and enjoy the celebratory mood, they ended up undertaking chores (I should have been doing) around the house as well as the bigger inconvenience of taking the time to visit me in hospital – not their idea of a fun break from the English weather!! Nurse Eileen from Rex became aware of the unfortunate timing of the two events and somehow under the cover of fading light, and wearing the usual attire for a raid of this type - blackened faces, night vision goggles, flak jackets etc., crept into my room and smuggled me away into the getaway vehicle – made to look like an ambulance (with flashing lights, no less) to join the party. 30 minutes later I was wheeled into the reception area only to find my son with a microphone in his hand saying, "Make a speech, come on Dad, just say a few words, and all I could muster was some kind of "ga-ga-bla-bla" noise. It was nothing like what I had rehearsed in my mind when I knew I would eventually make it to the event. Pathetic!

I didn't even get to sample the bubbly stuff (or I did and don't remember), but I think the fact that I went, even if I was horizontal for most of the time, made the exercise worthwhile and I shall be forever

grateful to Nurse Eileen and her co-conspirators for granting me that opportunity.

Neuro Fatigue:

At the time, I had no idea whether my constant tardiness was one of the direct symptoms of my stroke or whether it had something to do with those little "nurse-vampires" (as they were unaffectionately regarded) that come around in the (ridiculously) early hours of the morning, but always with a big smile as they wake you up with a greeting along the lines…, "Good morning Mr. Barton, my name is Julia and I just need to take a blood sample.." So many times I wanted to respond with, "Buggar off and go find somebody else! I have no more blood left to give.. Grrr!"

Regardless, I still found myself sleeping a huge amount of time with my days broken up around trips to the cafeteria and a therapy session or two.. I hated being so tired all the time.. Friends and family would visit and I would literally drop off during the conversation – so rude. On one occasion, one of my friends simply left a note for me to find.. "Just stopped by to see you but decided not want to wake you.. must go, luv ya!! xx". Even worse.. I missed out on my favorite (homemade) ice cream she brought me especially.

Hospital Therapy:

My (Inpatient) Physical Therapist was a gentleman by the name of Giovanni (AKA Gianni) Di Nuzio, PT. Prior to my first session with him, almost every nurse that checked my schedule said, "Ah, I see you have Gianni today.. he's definitely one of the best!" Another would say, "you know you are very lucky to have Gianni.." one Nurse after the other, it was nonstop praise (I don't know how much he paid them). I was beginning to think I was going to a circus with a Ringmaster bellowing out to the audience.. "And now for your pleasure... the one... the only.. THE.. GRRRRREAT.. GIOVANNI DI-NUZIO!!" (Crowd goes wild, that sort of thing).

Nevertheless, he was just the sort of guy that was best suited to my character.. Goodness, he "saw me coming".. I was disruptive, inconsiderate to the point of being rude and an overall *pain in the backside* – Gianni

was tough as old boots and gave back as good as he got! To the extent, at times, I sensed he was beginning to take pleasure with inflicting more and more pain on me in an effort to obtain some kind of physical reaction. I wanted to thump him, but the coward in me generally caused me to back down & soak it up and saved me from being expelled, which I am sure the other patients in the gym were hoping for. But if "physical therapy customer service" was measured by the principle of "the customer is always right", then in my mind and at that time, Gianni would have scored a negative 50! Benefitting from hindsight, I would now revise that score to a positive 200.

Regardless, I must acknowledge, however, that as a PT with little to no time to prepare a hopeless Stroke Survivor with a rotten attitude (like me) for the outside world, I could not have had anyone better.

Christy C, OTR/L managed my Occupational

Therapy needs, which were extensive. How does one shave, brush their teeth or get dressed when half your limbs are not functioning? Further, Christy was the first to determine that I failed to properly distinguish between hot and cold temperatures. It was only now, a few days after admittance that I was beginning to appreciate the enormity and challenges of the road ahead! Oh woe is me!

Speech pathology was under the direction of Ms. Diana M, SLP. I know I will never go down as one of her favorite patients since I was always looking for an excuse to tease her. When she asked if I was ready for my consult one

morning and I replied saying how tired I was.. She erroneously responded with, "That's ok, we can do it in bed if you like.." - imagine how much fun I had with that remark?!!

Diana was also responsible for determining whether her patient showed symptoms of dysphagia (difficulty with swallowing), as I understood it, no patient could be released from hospital if they suffered with

the condition, although it did occur to me that maybe this was a deliberate rumor spread around to make sure that we all ate the ghastly food we were encouraged to endure. Ordinarily, I love a Sunday family roast pork, but never again will I be able to enjoy apple sauce as the preferred condiment since the substance (in abundance) seemed to be the staple diet in the cafeteria – apple sauce and pills!

Diners:

The cafeteria happened to be located at the end of my ward and was aptly called "Diners" – each day seemed to go so fast with 3-4 therapy sessions along with the occasional visitor to see and just as I was enjoying a well-earned afternoon nap, Julie, the nurse on duty at around that time, would wake me and say.. "C'mon Sweet-pea, we need to get you ready for Diners". It appeared to me that 2013 was the "year of the Stroke" there seemed so many victims that gathered to eat at around 6pm each day – most seemed older and even more "crotchety" than me (no small feat) – I did not appreciate at the time, that some had lost their ability to speak which may have accounted for the sudden and hasty shuffling and maneuvering of wheelchairs closer together each time I was wheeled into the room which basically said to me.. "This table

is full mister, so Buggar off and find somewhere else!" Like me, most could not use their cutlery and required a nurse or a loved one to help spoon-feed them. Also, like me, most suffered with CMD –A medical condition that is more easily identified through the consumption of Apple Sauce (which HadyMed provided by the gallon). CMD (Corner Mouth Drool) happens when the mouth fails to seal completely – in my case, the left side was particularly vulnerable and so the napkin played a major role at meal times, even to this day, I suffer with CMD, although like many of my disabilities it is marginally better than it was, I am pleased to report.

The Hady-Med Nursing staff were truly fantastic and extremely tolerant of me and my antics, and fortunately for me, I got the impression there was no contractual clause that could allow them to send me back from where I came - Rex Hospital had previously learned their own lesson – no wonder they were so keen to sell me the benefits of HadyMed's Rehab capability and send me away in double-quick time!.

Striving For Perfection

I know God is up there, I speak to him every day, and most of the time, asking for forgiveness for abusing my one and only body so badly in the first place and despite him giving me a second chance, I have consistently failed to work hard, and diligently follow the professional and learned guidance as offered by my talented Therapists. Okay, so I am not perfect, but I am not sure he is either! Apparently, he created us (and other living creatures) on the sixth day of the seven he needed to create the whole universe – by today's standards, that's a Saturday! As a former Design Engineer, I can tell you I never did my best work on a Saturday – way too many distractions.. Saturday is (English) Football day it's Chill-out and Relax day, Play with the kids Day maybe even a Work in the Garden Day but never a Lets-do-A-Really-Complicated Design Day. And definitely not the day to be figuring out how the brain and its billions of cells should be sending signals to the body's muscles, don't you think?

Us Stroke Survivors have come to learn the hard way, that for every muscle (or group of muscles) we need to activate in order to move an arm or a leg, for example, at the exact same time, the brain has to tell another muscle (or group of muscles) to deactivate and be quiet, and without both signals meeting their objectives perfectly, you (and particularly the limb) is going nowhere! More specifically, the simple action of scratching one's nose requires the brain to fire the biceps muscle, in order to "curl" the arm and hand up toward the face and at that precise moment in time, the brain must send another signal to turn off the triceps' muscle which is there to straighten the arm (the opposite direction). If both muscles are firing at the same time, your arm will not bend and your neck is not long enough to make up the difference (well

mine isn't). I won't bore you with the amount and type of muscles that need to fire or turn off to move the fingers – way too many to mention.

Now most of us (more elementary) Designers follow the KISS (Keep It Simple Stupid) principles of design – for starters: less is (usually) better.

Had Orville and Wilbur been working on a Saturday, Today's Airline pilots may have had to control 2 sets of elevators simultaneously - one for taking off and the other for landing and if one set was not fully deactivated we would never leave (or arrive at) the airport! Thank goodness, The Wright Brothers and most Aeronautical Engineers work normal hours.

There's No Place Like Home:

Before a Stroke Patient can be released from the hospital they must obtain the full support of the medical professionals that make up the team monitoring his/her progress.

In my case, Alison McCartney, CCM., was my Case Leader and she would meet regularly with the team of professionals (which would include, Dr. Harris, select nursing staff from the ward and representatives from the PT,OT & SLP departments) and from those meetings she could then determine an approximate release date. After 2 months at HadyMed, at least in my mind, I was ready to go home, and having learned the importance of Alison's role in the decision process caused me to quiz her at every opportunity possible - a bit like the child in the car, "are we there yet?", and like the adult in the same analogy, Alison would become more and more agitated

and brutally honest with her responses, hoping, I am sure, I would shut up and leave her alone. "Maybe when you can take a pee when and where you should, maybe then we could consider it!" she once said.

Finally, the day came when Alison gave me the great news that I could go home the following Friday – I am not sure I understood at the time why there was dancing in the wards and beaming grins on the faces of all the nurses when they heard the news. Of course, I understand now! The discharge date was made even better because Andy Murray was on his way to the Wimbledon Final to be played 3 days later. He won, beating Djokovic and becoming the first British guy to hoist the trophy since Fred Perry in 1936. Fantastic and I got to see it! Thank you, Hady-Med!

'Til Death Do Us Part:

Prior to my final departure, Christy C took the opportunity to visit our house and with her trained eye, pointed out those areas that required modification of some kind – the provision of a hand-rail or two and so on. I was still dependent on my wheelchair,

so most of the doors had to be removed and in some cases, whole doorways widened. Fortunately, my sister, Debs and her husband Jim remained after the wedding to help with some of the repairs and modifications recommended.

Christy was also largely responsible for training Sarah as my future, (resident) Caregiver – particularly the techniques necessary for transferring me from my wheelchair to the dinner table, the bed or into the car and so on.

We were most fortunate to have a very special group of friends and family who in the first instance, donated to a fund to help with initial and exceptional expenses needed for my return to home life. This was gratefully accepted, afterall, by the time I left the hospital, we were flat broke!

Luckily for me, the U-14 Soccer team I used to coach some years previously had all become "strapping lads", and one of the parents (and the team's photographer), Lewis Midyette, kindly offered to organize them and set up a working party for a weekend to build a wheelchair ramp to his design for me to

access the house from the driveway. When I think of all the miserable fitness drills I made them do despite the weather – I was extremely humbled to see them all from my window with tools

in one hand and a .plank of wood over their shoulder – all for my benefit. The true meaning of "*tough love*", I suppose.

New Doctor and Therapist referrals were lined up and one of Sarah's first tasks was to set up appointments and ferry me to and from the various locations.

I would require a number of Out-Patient medical follow ups and high up the list was out-patient PT and OT (physical and occupational therapies), to continue the work started by Gianni and Christy

at HadyMed, so I was referred to Steps For Recovery in Cary (normally, about a 30 minute drive). It is strange to think that all the times that I sat in Sarah's car, never before did I notice how fast she drove, but now, a minute could not go by without me having to make some kind of derogatory comment (or three).. "Slow down!"; or "there's no rush!"; "where's the fire?"; "Have your waters broken or something else I should know?".. Even when we left with loads of time to spare, we always seemed to be in a hurry! Of course, she denied it claiming that it was my imagination and that she was driving responsibly and well under the speed limit. I think part of it was to do with my limited muscle control that had me rocking to and fro' and side to side. When on the odd occasion that my daughter, Hannah, substituted, I found that she was just as fast so I guess it was my lack of judgement, afterall, so best shut up before I get thrown in the trunk – gagged and strapped to the wheelchair!"

Shutting up was a new skill I had to learn and accept.. Ultimately I was no longer capable of doing the tasks that previously were so simple.. Driving a car, odd jobs around the house, paying the bills, making appointments and so on.. I could not

even be trusted to take my pills when I should, I may be home but I was pretty useless - so poor old Sarah would have to step up and take on a whole load of new responsibilities in addition to being the primary caregiver and sole bread-earner...I am sure there have been many times she wanted to take back the bit about, "till death do us part"!

Out Patient Needs:

Katie Stephens PT,NCS would become my Physical Therapist at Steps For Recovery, and with her husband, Josh Olinick, they owned and managed the Practice and were highly respected and well known to the HadyMed group, they also followed the same discipline and techniques associated with the "Neuro-Ifrah" approach to physical therapy for Brain (and spinal cord) injury Survivors. Even after all this time, I am still not totally sure how this particular therapy technique differed from others.. Particularly for those like me, suffering with hemiparesis (weakness to my left side limbs), but from experience, the following observations come to mind.. "Show little to no sympathy"; "Ten must never be the last number in a set of strenuous exercise reps, Ten is only the trigger for another set"; and most important, "pain proves feeling". At my first meeting and consult, Katie cautioned me that it could be a long process and indeed, when I asked how long the treatment may take, she was the first of the many Stroke Rehab Specialists to respond with the immortal phrase (that I did not want to hear).. "I honestly don't know, everybody's Stroke is different!" .. As did Ann-Marie Alliano, the Steps' Occupational Therapist on my first meeting with her.

Diana H SLP, my hospital (and first) Speech Pathologist, referred me to Maura English Silverman MS, CCC/SLP, a lady very much in demand, but fortunately for me, managed to squeeze me into her busy schedule. She also had an office at the Steps' facility which saved another journey and more of Sarah's driving, phew!

Maura had founded and ran the local charity, *Triangle Aphasia Project* (TAP) - an internationally recognized and highly respected organization which consumed a huge amount of her time. As I have come to learn, I was really lucky that I did not suffer with (full-blown) Aphasia (deterioration of communication skills – particularly, loss of speech and diminished comprehension) (usually affecting those where the brain injury impacted the left side of their brain), my speech issues were confined to the time of the actual event itself and by the time I was settled in rehab hospital, I was reasonably fluent and coherent, I did exhibit some (right-side-brain injury) deficits like dyscalculia and dysgraphia (difficulties with simple arithmetic calculations and grammar in written composition, respectively) and apparently, I was quite stoic – I suffered really badly with "left-side neglect" (lack of attention and impaired spatial awareness to my left side). My organizational skills were practically non-existent; I really struggled with the most basic time sensitive tasks.

Upon reflection, I think my "Queen's English" accent did me no favors.. Many of the medical professionals upon

Simon could always tell when he was beginning to lose his audience

Simon never told his wife that when he was fit enough, he planned to run away with his massage therapist, Samantha

first meeting me, I felt, thought I was way more intelligent than I actually was! But in fairness to that profession, much of my past (US-wide) career achievements can be attributed to the same over-estimation.

I used to undertake many technical lectures and when I started to speak, the audience anticipated significantly higher degrees of technicality and overall expertise than they actually ended up with - leaving them quite relieved when I finally finished.

In addition to the usual and accepted rehab therapies and on our own volition, we decided to seek out a good Chiropractor – 3 months on a hospital bed with very little exercise had taken its toll – my back was in bad shape and my left shoulder was so sore it took Samantha Newton, Steps' resident Massage Therapist, an intensely laborious 1 hour of treatment just to enable the OT to begin work on my arm and hand.

A friend of ours recommended Dr. Mike Hoehle of Raleigh Chiropractic & Wellness – The X-ray he took of my spine, prior to treatment, revealed the inherent deformity and confirmed the action needed – he was a young chap and built like an American Footballer, he took great pleasure in showing his strength and particularly when it came to the unavoidable spine & neck crack (that so many in his profession like to do) at the end of the session, although I think in my case, he gave the "snap" procedure a little more *gusto* than usual - which I am sure was largely due to my constant "ribbing".. suggesting that compared to Rugby, American Football was a game for whimps and panzies! (afterall, why else would they wear Kevlar armor and a helmet and get to sit on the sidelines for most of the game? I would say). It would take around 20 sessions of manipulation as well as a tailored exercise program at home to get it back to any degree of normalcy. "Now Simon, put your left leg over there, your right arm down there.. And most important.. RELAX!" (yeah right - easy to say, but I know what's about to come). It was a good thing that I could not drive, when I left his office, I felt quite "floaty" a little drunk even! My insurance did not cover his services but despite the cost, it was definitely worth it.

Further, he kindly collaborated with Katie at Steps For Recovery to ensure he was working within the realms of those areas she had targeted for improvement.

By around my 5th visit with Katie she had me getting up from a sitting position to standing relatively comfortably and then one day, with her sat on a "wheelie-stool" next to me she carefully encouraged and guided me, one step at a time, and before I knew it, I was actually walking across the room! This was met with a rush of emotion and I could not help but cry for joy – literally tears rolling down my cheeks. . It is extraordinary to think, as adults, how we take the simple act of walking, for granted – it had seemed like an eternity since I last walked without assistance – a moist eye was more than justified, in my opinion . Sadly, excessive bouts of emotion did not stop there. To this day, it does not take much to make me cry or giggle uncontrollably. Apparently, PBA (Pseudo Bulbar Affect) is not an uncommon condition following a brain injury. Although I must admit, whilst it is nice to use the excuse of a medical condition, frankly, I was turning into a whimpering old fart pre-stroke anyhow. The Little House On the Prairie along with hero award type ceremonies are TV programs I must avoid at all costs!!

More Than Meets The Eye:

After a while, Katie felt that my physical therapy could be improved if I sought the intervention of a Vision Specialist - and preferably, one whose expertise was in the area of neuro-optometry. Accordingly, she recommended I see Dr. Nancy Mackowsky, a highly regarded Professional and relatively local. It was felt that any future progress could be enhanced through regaining

some spatial awareness which in turn, would help overall balance. Diana M at HadyMed was the first to point out, during my stay at Rehab Hospital, that I was exhibiting clear signs of "Left Side Neglect" and she, like Maura (as did all the Professionals) would be constantly reminding me to look in their direction when talking – of course, they deliberately chose to sit to my left to emphasize the point. But the condition really showed itself when one day, following a meal, Sarah asked me to look at my plate and literally only half the food was eaten (the empty side of the plate, to my right, was clean as a whistle).

Of course, as it stood, and in my current condition, there would be no opportunity to ever drive a car again.. Just using the Supermarket's courtesy motorized cart would see me crashing into the food shelves – not to mention the occasional customer along the way. Driving a car safely was something we all wanted for me to achieve – the sooner the better!

My first appointment at The Mackowsky Visual Learning and Rehabilitation Clinic started with an eye exam, and not the simple "characters on a wallchart" type exam but one that would identify the many shortfalls and weaknesses evident resulting from the type of brain injury I suffered. Spatially, I was quite a disaster, I thought, but Dr. Mackowsky still agreed to take me on.. . She did not think me a complete "lost cause"! (Lucky me).

Despite the fact that every visit I had at Dr, Mackowsky's clinic emphasized my visual deficiencies, I did find the work (and homework assignments she gave) challenging but quite satisfying.. Some of the tasks were quite weird and often involved the combination of both eye and physical exercise simultaneously. There was not a single area in our kitchen that didn't have a place for me to practice something. But based on the results of the subsequent exams, and with her prescription for new (prism inclusive) glasses, tangible and significant improvements had been made. Who would have thought that one's vision could influence your ability to simply stand with equal weight to both feet? So now I could approach the physical therapy work with Katie with a little more renewed vigor and purpose resulting from a little better feedback with tangible progress being made.

I should point out that during these early weeks, I was still wearing the same AFO (Ankle Foot Orthosis) I was fitted in Rehab hospital this was due to "Foot Drop", simply, I could not seem to activate the muscles to the

side and front of my shin bone (Tibialis Anterior) responsible for raising the foot and at the same time, deactivate my Soleus (the larger, calf muscle) whose primary function is to point the foot down. This would mean that without AFO support I would be vulnerable to "dropping" and dragging the foot which could cause me to trip and fall. Katie tried anything and everything to stimulate the muscles and get them to fire, this included scratching the toes, tickling the underside of the foot, electrocution (AKA, "E-Stim"), but nothing seemed to do the job.

I did progress onto a more advanced AFO – carbon graphite version - much sleeker and more lightweight and so as time moved on my walking became a little more confident and steady.

Kristin Nuchols took over my Occupational Therapy needs from Ann-Marie – this involved many hours of work on my left arm and hand.

Apparently, the arm and hand are notoriously difficult to recover following Stroke and it is easy to see why.. We use our lower limbs much more (outside the treatment room), just the simple act of sitting down, for example, forces us to use our leg muscles just to balance ourselves whereas our upper limbs require less common reasons to be used, particularly as your good arm and hand starts to dominate, and with the absence of a regular, repetitive exercise, it becomes harder for the brain to rewire those connections that became damaged.

Katy and Kristin would encourage the use of a mirror for the purposes of gaining some visual feedback to the brain. I found that I hated looking at myself in the mirror, largely because I didn't recognize the (much uglier) person looking back at me (for starters, my facial "droop" was still evident) – and with the absence of any movement at all, I would soon became quite demotivated - I was sure that if I could move one of those affected limbs, just a fraction, it would have encouraged me to work harder –particularly at home, but in fairness to Katy and Kristin, they had the great misfortune, having me as a patient!

Ain't Got Rhythm:

I was referred to Dr. Deepak Pasi, Cardiologist at North Carolina Heart & Vascular to see if my heart problem that caused the stroke could be resolved once and for all.. Despite the severity of the condition and the concern it carried, a visit to Dr. Pasi's office was usually quite a pleasant experience – he always welcomed you with the biggest smile – Deep down though, I was concerned he might be one of those "Smiling Assassins" you hear about! But for the most part, he was generally laid back and upbeat about the whole thing – a very calming influence – clearly, he had seen it all before.. Following a battery of tests (mainly EKG's and Echo-cardiograms) it was clear that my heart beat remained irregular which sadly, remains to this day,

Although more recently, my "A-Fibrillation" had somehow morphed into an "A-Flutter" (irregular and very fast) – Dr. Pasi confirmed that I suffered with a condition called "Hypertrophic Cardiomyopathy" – it took me a long time to learn how to say that let alone spell it! It means, as I understand it, that I likely inherited a condition where the lower wall of the left ventricle is thicker than normal which reduces pumping efficiency and indirectly, can mess with the heart's electrical system and beat regularity.. And if the blood does not evacuate the heart properly it can pool and clot making the potential of a stroke a greater possibility. Sadly the condition is not easily curable without major surgery so the preferred course of action is to treat the symptoms. Thinning the blood so that it cannot clot is the first and biggest precaution. The thought of being on blood thinning pills for the rest of my life is not a prospect I was looking forward to but if the alternative was another stroke – I will take the pills! That said, I was given a Cardioversion, quite a scary procedure where they zap (electrocute) the heart in an effort to reset it and get it back into normal rhythm. Allegedly, on one occasion immediately following one jolt and despite my comatose condition, I managed to sit up and fire off a few expletives which

were quite English and colorful in nature but left the nursing staff a little bewildered to the extent that when I came around, I was asked to translate (I am not sure they were glad they asked, I know I regretted telling) (sorry, but I have no intention of sharing with you here either!).

Driving For Independence:

Largely due to Dr. Mackowsky's fine work, we felt confident enough for me to get behind the wheel again. My son, Luke was the perfect choice to sit beside me for the following reasons.. He was available, he was

brave (and slightly stupid) and most important, he was extremely patient and tolerant – particularly when my pride would get in the way - which was quite often – more so when considering that Luke did not have an **unblemished** driving record himself, and with the obvious age difference, it was quite easy for me to react negatively to his advice when given!

Other than the difficulty of maintaining focus for long periods of time, after a few weeks' practice, I was sure I could take a driving test and pass. As it happens, I did take a test and subsequently failed! A momentary lapse of concentration was cited as the primary reason.

Pigs Might Fly:

I spent way too much time watching (and falling asleep in front of) the television and when there was not much to see then I would check out YouTube and find a documentary (or three) – My cousin Tim had recently completed a personal biography and tribute to our Grandfather and his life in the Royal Flying Corps during the early years of the (Great) First World War and this caused me to become fascinated (to the point of obsession) with that period in history.. And on one occasion when I had seen all there was to see, I found myself investigating Stroke treatments when I happened across a short documentary by the 60-Minutes' Investigation team relating to the work discovered and offered by The Institute of Neurological Recovery (INR) based in Florida. Dr. Edward Tobinick had discovered that by injecting the drug, Etanercept (commercially known as Enbrel), into the patient's spinal veins (around the back of the neck area) it could provide a positive neurological effect. The particular episode I saw featured a lady (a former school teacher) that suffered a Stroke 3 years previously that left her unable to speak and the program followed her undergoing the treatment and miraculously, immediately following the procedure, her speech returned and her motor functions improved dramatically. Naturally, I became very excited about the potential and through the generosity of my mother, raised the money to obtain an appointment – C'mon; it had to be worth a try. In searching the web for further background information and reviews the INR was typically "slammed" from many so-called "professionals" with one (televised on the same documentary) when asked if the treatment could be beneficial, responded with "well I suppose it's possible" quickly adding.. "… and pigs might fly.."

So did it cure me of all my ailments? No, of course not and neither was I promised to be "restored" to any extent. But did I benefit from the procedure? Absolutely! .. My shoulder pain completely disappeared immediately following the treatment and better still, just one week later, driving the same car, doing the same route with the same Examiner, I passed my driving test with him commenting to Sarah when we returned.. "it was like he was a different person!"

"Nudge-nudge; wink-wink; oink- oink!" (I say).

Back To Work:

My sudden departure from the business I founded placed an enormous strain on the remaining personnel, and particularly those that took on the obligation for meeting payroll and monthly overheads, mostly because they never had

"...as to the cost of the loan, Mr. Barton, is your other arm and leg in good working order?"

to endure that level of responsibility before, it was made worse because the business was growing at an unsustainable rate and simply, there was not enough access to cash – from me personally or any of the conventional sources. My eldest son, Josh, along with the VP of Engineering, Mike, took up the mantle as best they could, trying to get projects out the door, sales receipts in and minimize funds going out.

Sadly, my business could not be regarded as a great cash model.. Single sales orders were quite large, in the region of $200-800K each, and despite the excellent margins, sales were sporadic and too infrequent to inject the sort of cash needed for those "lull periods" between sales and particularly if there were additional and unforeseen expenses like a problem with manufactured quality or a delivery delay. Accordingly, we could go 3-4 months with no income at all. We needed more funds and despite the guys approaching every lender they could find (even the dubious ones), my useless credit (which was worsening by the day) inevitably resulted in silly offers with crazy payback terms. Both Josh and Mike were feeling the strain and I felt I had to get back to work urgently. With the benefit of hindsight, this proved to be a huge mistake; I was nowhere near mentally fit enough.

The Cyber Conspiracy:

For the longest time I thought there was some kind of conspiracy against me to make me look even more stupid than I actually was! When I came out of hospital all previously familiar technology was

no longer the same. At some point, Sarah felt the need to change to an alternative TV Service Provider which meant a different Remote Control to the one I remembered and at work; they said there was a need to upgrade various software on my personal computer – the Windows operating system, Microsoft office programs as well as my favorite 3D Design Modelling program. I struggled with the most basic stuff – a basic spreadsheet, composing a letter – I couldn't even work out how to draw a simple rectangle without having to ask one of the Engineers for assistance. Accordingly, my return to work was not as positive a contribution as I would have liked - quite the opposite actually, I started to sense the rolling of eyes as I was wheeled through the door. Not that I noticed at the time, but this discomfort was an indicator that I was not really ready to return to work (despite my desire and enthusiasm). All I really achieved was to cause inconvenience and worse still, I was making irrational decisions and getting into destructive arguments with people I cared about, and despite their animated and very justified concerns, I seemed incapable of listening. I can honestly say, my haste to return to work would be the primary cause of the company's eventual demise – a business I was very proud to build – in the process, my poor judgement also almost cost our house of 30 years. It took just 9 months before my (Chartered Accountant) brother, Nigel, persuaded me, that there was no hope in continuing and that the business, me and Sarah, had to file for bankruptcy, the sooner the better!

There was really no way out – a truly awful period of my life! It was made worse that from then on, Sarah would not only have the strain of being my Primary Caregiver at the same time as working her 40 hours per week serving undeserving airline customers but she would also have to meet and pay the bills with no income contribution from me!

Rock Bottom's Up:

I had no income, my business (along with any illusions of a prosperous retirement) seemed an impossible fantasy, my left arm, hand and leg were still knackered and non-functional, and I was still dependent on blood thinners because my heart condition had not improved. But heck, compared to many, these hick-ups were minimal, quite tolerable and not worth getting upset about.

My son Josh and his wife, Laura organized a party.. There is a popular party game designed to help the guests mingle - it involves a name on a label stuck to your back and out of view (except to others) - it is usually a well-known name and the idea is for each guest to go around asking only a limited number of "yes./no" questions of the others in an effort to be able to determine one's identity – the first to guess correctly wins a prize – you get the idea.. Typical names could be Mickey Mouse or Mohammed Ali or Jane Austin, Jesus Christ and so on, so questions may include.. "Am I alive or dead?", "man or woman" or, "am I fiction or real?" of course, being the slowest in the room I was getting more and more frustrated as everyone else were guessing their names but I had no clue about mine.. They chose to label me, "GRANDPA". So when they finally put me out of my misery, I cried – I was going to be a grandfather! Life is not so bad, afterall, wow.

Shortly afterward, I got myself over to the Social Security offices and was told that all the taxes I had paid over the years along with my various impairments did entitle me to a reasonable, monthly disability allowance – not a great sum, but enough to help keep the Bailiff away and with Sarah's income we would get by.

It took a while, but Sarah eventually persuaded me that with the kids all grown up and doing their thing we could downsize and by moving into a much smaller (ranch style type) house we could live quite comfortably and well within our means to the extent that we could have a few dollars left over by the end of each month.

My former VP of Engineering, Mike, came over my house one Sunday and asked me for my daughter's (Hannah's) hand in marriage since the collapse of my business, Mike managed to land himself a very good position with a local and highly respected engineering company – and was already making a good impression, of course, I cried as I said "she's all yours" to him with very little hesitation..

Things were definitely looking up!

The fact that I was driving a car helped with my independence and much less reliance on Sarah.

Mentors and The Grumpy Cripples Club.

Life continued to get better.. On alternate Thursdays I would attend the "Back To Work" Group organized by Maura and the Triangle Aphasia Project (TAP). I found that this "group" therapy meeting to be the single biggest help to my cognitive recovery - more than any other activity I have undertaken, post stroke. The group is made up of people that are, communicatively, at a higher level than the average TAP client to the extent that they are considering returning to the workplace but could do with a little more support and strategy and fine tuning of their communication & organizational skills. I have (and continue to be) inspired by those around the table. In the first place it provides added perspective on the nature and severity of my own issues and progress by providing tangible confirmation of how lucky I really was that my injury was confined to a relatively small region to the right side of my brain and secondly, without exception, I am always impressed by the self-motivation and bloody-minded determination the others possess (way more than me) to improve themselves along with their self-deprecating humor.. Better still, some have even been known to laugh at my jokes! Most evenings I would walk away with a smile and more of a spring in my step. So imagine my dejection and disappointment on the next Thursday when the group did not meet – the perfect opportunity for maybe meeting up at the local pub perhaps? So the Grumpy Cripples Club was formed.

Shawn F:

I actually met Shawn for the first time during a physical therapy session at HadyMed Hospital - he stopped in to say hello to the same therapists I was working with, Gianni and Christy – he was there just 5 months before me. I remember seeing him with a big smile on his face because he had just passed his (return to) driving exam and was enjoying his newly found independence. Frankly, at the time, I didn't know what all the fuss was about – until, later on, of course, when it was my turn!. But unlike me, from day 1, Shawn suffered with Aphasia and equally unlike me, he refused to let his condition get the better of him and displayed a determination to recover in the shortest possible time to the extent that he often found himself alone when he refused to leave the gym at the end of the therapy session.

Shawn was part of a group of guys that played ice hockey regularly at the local rink. It so happened during a game that one of his opponents hit him in the neck with their stick (right on Shawn's carotid artery, apparently, he said later, that the actual incident did not concern him at the time and carried on playing (remarkably) thinking nothing of it and it was only in the early hours of the following morning on a visit to the bathroom that his wife, Elizabeth, found him collapsed on the floor. In his case, the damage caused to his artery resulted in an (ischemic) stroke, and because it was to the left side of his brain, his speech was impacted enormously to the extent that during his stay in rehab hospital, his wife and daughters could barely understand a word (he would try to say).

On one occasion, Shawn and Elizabeth invited Sarah and me over to their house for dinner one evening.. It was a new house on a new subdivision, so new that the GPS did not recognize the address at all and we got hopelessly lost so I pulled over and called Shawn

from my mobile phone, the conversation went like this..

"Shawn, sorry mate but we are going to be late we are lost with no idea which way to go!"

"Where are you?" He replied, "..And I will talk you through the rest of the way".

We are on Wait Avenue at the intersection of South Franklyn Street (to our right)".

Okay he said, I can see you on the map.. so keep driving East and about half a mile up you will turn left at the lights on North Allen, then go down the hill and turn right on Jupiter." Now Shawn was still prone to the occasional slurred word and added to the fact that he had already made a start on the Sangria, I was not totally sure I heard correctly so for clarification, decided to repeat back to him..

"Okay, so left on North Allen then watch out for a turning to my right, called Jupiter, Jupiter - like the planet! Right?", I said for added emphasis, "Yes, go down North Allen and turn right on Juniper avenue", "Oh I'm sorry" I quickly corrected myself, "turn right on Juniper, Juniper - like the berry!" Yes, Jupiter" he responded, "Jupiter, like the planet? I asked again, "Yes, Juniper", "Juniper, like the berry!" "Yes, Jupiter" and so it went on and on.. "Juniper?" "Jupiter!"; "Jupiter?" "Juniper!" We were going nowhere fast so I quickly said thanks and hung up. Sarah said, "So what did he say?" I said, "we are going up here and then we are going to turn left on North Allen, then we will look for a street beginning with the letter 'J' and we will turn right on it! Then **you** will call him back for more instructions!" "Well okay," she said.

We actually made it somehow (albeit much later than the designated time), Shawn met us as we approached the door and with a glass of Sangria in his hands, said, "do you want a drink?"

David H :

David was also a victim of a left-side-brain stroke, and like me, it was "ischemic", apparently resulting from some kind of hole in his heart that caused the embolus (blood clot type blockage) and resulting brain injury.

As with Shawn and me, David found himself a bit of a loose-end every other Thursday and so became another enthusiastic founder member of the GCC.

One time he ordered Soup with his beer and when the waiter came around with the pepper-mill he suddenly burst out laughing, I asked him what was so funny he replied " ah.. it was just

another example of my wretched conductive aphasia and where I am prone to mishearing things.. "you saw the Waiter leaning over to me, right? Well I thought he said, 'a little pecker, Sir?'"

June B:

AKA "Mum", Somewhere in this book I had to find a place to pay tribute to my mother.. Mum is from that generation where it was regarded poor form to complain or whine about your ailment... An example of one of those really great "put down" lines was, "quit moaning, it doesn't hurt, look at your Great Uncle Stan.. he was bombed in the First World War and had his head completely blown off, and do you know? He never said a word!"

For the past 15 years or more, my mum has been battling with one form of cancer or another, just when we thought she beat the thing, it morphed and went somewhere else in her body, creating a new set of ugly symptoms to contend with – not the way to be spending your "fourth quarter". With me living so far away, I was unable to provide much in the way

of comfort or care-giving.. That responsibility fell with my 3 siblings but that did not stop me from making a Sunday afternoon telephone call. In the early days I thought by initiating the call I was doing it for her but I cannot deny I was the true beneficiary of the chat. So often I could feel a bit low with my own set of woes but in true form she could still (metaphorically) "slap" me around the face and bring me to my senses by reminding me that I really did not have much to complain about. These calls were (and still are) great psychological therapy.. It did occur to me that she could provide me an additional revenue stream by providing her telephone number and a $50/hour consult to anyone that that thinks they are having a hard time! I would even provide a guarantee that she will cure you during those weak moments!

Andy E :

Andy was relatively new to the area and was introduced to the TAP clients as an author of his own book relating to his personal stroke recovery experience.. I can confirm, having purchased my own (autographed) copy, it is a really great read, beautifully written and unlike this one, very instructional and beneficial to the Stroke Survivor & Caregiver.. As he became aware of my own efforts, Andy kindly made time to give me some invaluable pointers. His book is entitled, "Dangers Of Pimento Cheese" (he was half way through eating a pimento cheese sandwich when he experienced his right-hemi Stroke). ... Not suggesting for a second that the ingredients were contributory to the unfortunate event – I respectfully suggest that without hesitation, you purchase, read and enjoy.

Splish Splash I was taking a shower!:

On a trip to England last year, Sarah and I were invited to stay overnight with some old friends, Mike and Delia, a nice house, but not one designed around the "mobility impaired" (like me)... After showing our bedroom, Delia told us that we were welcome to use the shower over the bathtub – Sarah took one look and in her protective mind and with dagger-eyes for added reinforcement she said to me.. "Don't even think of getting in there by yourself! – I will help you!". In the middle of the night I took my customary bathroom break and as I sat on the loo I could not help but notice that the back corner of the bath had quite a large flat surface area - and I concluded that it was big enough for me to place my big bum there and simply swing my legs over and into the tub, and after a brief moment to poise myself I could then stand up and walk the couple of steps to the front end, close the curtain and operate the shower head and when I was done.. Simply reversing the procedure will allow me to get out – "easy-peasy-lemon-squeezy!"

I woke up first that morning and decided to let Sarah enjoy a rare lie-in, I can certainly brush my teeth on my own and now that I have determined a cunning plan to get in and out of the bathtub there was absolutely no reason to disturb her, I felt – Gosh, I may even gain a couple of brownie points which will set me up well for the rest of the day!

I snuck out of the bedroom and managed to get into the bathroom without making a sound – so all looked good. After brushing my teeth and stripping down, as envisaged, I perched my bottom on the corner of the bath, swung my legs over and I was set. Unfortunately, my plan failed to appreciate how slippery the base of the bath was nor did I see the slight downward slope that went from back to front. Forget walking to the front end.. I could not have been standing 2 seconds before my feet shot out from underneath me. I thought that I managed to stifle the "whoa" cry and that the thudding sound of my back hitting the porcelain was negligible at worst, but 30 seconds could not have passed before Sarah was standing over me with her "You Are Dead-look", of course I had nothing on but a big frown of humiliation.. which became even more pronounced by the knock on the door and Delia on the other side saying, "is everything alright in there?", Sarah managed to prise my arms up and away from being wedged between my body and the sides of the bath.. Up to that point I was totally immobile - Not that it helped much, with the absence of a structurally sound hand rail to grab, my contribution was limited to using the soap dish for leverage which very easily came away in my hand. Sarah would pull and I would push, we would get to around half way out when I could not help but burst into hysterical laughter which would cause her to let go in despair and so I simply slipped back in – pretty much the exact spot as before. After about 5 more goes and 10 minutes later but with the added aid of an extra pair of (Delia's) hands, I was out! As you might have gathered I earned ZERO brownie points that day!

In case you were wondering, there are three reasons why I added this little tale near the end of my story.. First, I had actually finished the first draft of the book last week but a couple of days ago I was watching one of 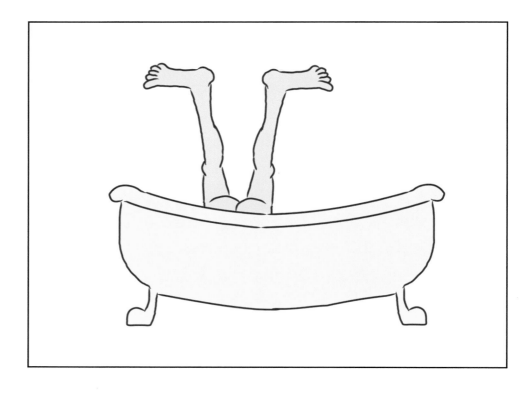 those David Attenborough wildlife documentaries which focused on Elephant Seals launching themselves off the ice into the arctic water somewhere, which reminded me of the event. Second, it was one of those important life lessons which said.. "you are making progress but NOT to the extent of getting cocky" and last, I had hoped this book be represented by a "feel-good" story allowing the reader to leave it with a smile on their face – or even better, a feeling of.. "well at least I am not as bad as him!" ..

I promise, you don't have to look far to find someone a little worse off than you!

7.1 Moving Forward With Optimism:

After the failure of my business and my contribution to its downfall along with my physical weaknesses I decided I would not seek employment somewhere else or at least not until I had the confidence to apply when I knew for sure, I really was the best person for the job and in that regard, Sarah helped me set up a little engineering consultancy/home office business which has allowed me the time to write this memoir as well as practice and maintain my engineering skills. My little biz has progressed very nicely to the extent that quite soon, I will be letting Uncle Sam know they can take me off the monthly disability allowance that has helped keep the roof over our heads! This has meant that our house is still ours to sell and downsize sometime in the future so maybe we can reconsider the likelihood of a comfortable retirement afterall – something we both thought was unlikely just a couple of years ago when we believed we hit rock-bottom. This new sense of purpose, I am sure, has contributed to a better overall attitude which has not only seen a massive cognitive improvement but physically, my left side continues to get better. Gardening and a little golf is just on the horizon, I am sure!

But Sarah, if you are reading this – please don't get ahead of yourself.. As implied on the first page.. I really don't want those trousers back! (Particularly as you have worn them so well).

My average day (7 days per week) starts with a reasonably intense physical stretching exercise followed by a light breakfast and then I lock myself away in my office to write or do engineering work.. Two mornings per week I try to get in a professional (physical) therapy session of some kind, I have since been referred to Allied Therapy in Wake Forest for both PT and OT - it is quite local and with an early appointment I can get there and back without disrupting my office work too badly. My walking remains strong and confident, indeed, I have participated in a couple of (relatively long) charity walks with no concerns. I now have a lot more controlled movement in my arm and although I still type with one hand, every day, my left hand's spasticity eases and it won't be long before one of the fingers will help by holding down the shift key, at least, I am sure.

I have come to adopt Winston Churchill's philosophy (I think it was him) that when I climb into bed at the end of the day and before drifting off to sleep – I take the time first to reflect on the day and how productive I have been and second, consider tomorrow and what I can do to be even better. My only worry is that sometimes I get so excited about what I can do tomorrow that it has caused me, on occasion, to stoop so low as to set the alarm clock thus reducing the risk of over-sleeping. Sometimes, I need to make the day as long as possible to cram everything in. This is a thin and precarious line I am treading, afterall; I hope I am not going back to the old Simon again! (I don't much care for him anymore).

As I come to the close of my story which has now been a year in the making and nearly five years after the actual stroke event itself, I think I am now better qualified to answer the question posed at the beginning of this book and often raised by most survivors of stroke.. "so, when will I recover?" And despite my mocking of the medical profession's boilerplate ["everybody's stroke is different"] response, I must first acknowledge that their answer is quite fair afterall, I only have to look at my (stroke survivor) friends to see the difference in their own ranges and rates of progress.

I can only conclude that for me, I have learned not to be wasting so much time trying to recover to where I once was – I found that the more I strived for that target the more unattainable it was and the more frustrated and depressed I became, but rather focus my energy more on my new self and work as best I can with what I have – which is a lot more than many, thank you very much and have a nice day!

--- END---

Printed in the United States
By Bookmasters